NETWORK
BEYOND BIAS

MAKING DIVERSITY A COMPETITIVE ADVANTAGE FOR YOUR CAREER

COMPANION WORKBOOK

From the author of *Network Beyond Bias*

Amy C. Waninger

Printed in the United States of America

First Printing, 2019

ISBN: 978-1-720794-82-0

Lead at Any Level, LLC
13009 Fairfax Ct
Fishers, IN 46055
www.LeadAtAnyLevel.com

Ordering Information:
Quantity sales. Special discounts are available on quantity purchases by corporations, associations, and others who purchase directly from the publisher. Contact amy@LeadAtAnyLevel.com for details.

Bring this program to your organization:
Lead at Any Level, LLC works with organizations that want to build diverse leadership bench strength for a sustainable competitive advantage. Contact amy@LeadAtAnyLevel.com for booking information.

Our Brains Are Biased

Which of these categories seems most relevant to you? Why?

_____

_____

_____

_____

_____

Which of these categories seems least important to you? Why?

_____

_____

_____

_____

Where Does Bias Come From?

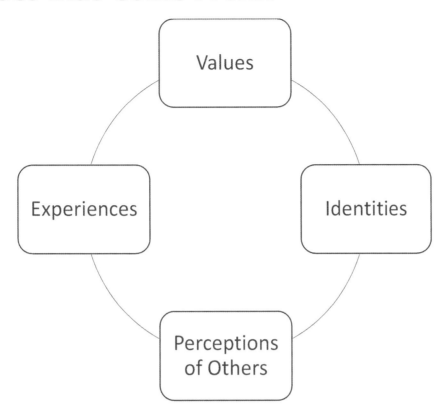

List some of your most cherished values.

_____

_____

_____

What identity or identities do these values support and protect?

_____

_____

_____

How do you perceive others who do not share these values and/or identities?

_____

_____

_____

What experiences do you choose that reinforce your values, identity, and perceptions of others?

_____

_____

_____

What experiences could you undertake that might challenge or broaden your point of view?

_____

_____

_____

What, in your opinion, makes someone a "good person"?

_____

_____

_____

Move Beyond Unconscious Bias

1. Put yourself on _____.

2. _____ the responses of others.

3. Press your _____.

Which of these steps is easiest for you? Which is most difficult? Why do you think that is?

_____

_____

_____

_____

_____

_____

_____

_____

Notes

Break the Cycle of Unconscious Bias

Think about something that happened recently, such as learning about a change at work or encountering a new person or situation.

1. **What did you notice about yourself?**

What were your feelings?		What values drove your feelings?		Which of your identities is involved?
_____	←	_____	←	_____
_____	←	_____	←	_____
_____	←	_____	←	_____
_____	←		←	

2. What responses did you observe from others?

_____

_____

_____

_____

3. Press your Pause Button. What response is most productive?

_____

_____

Now think about another situation that caused a very different reaction for you.

1. **What did you notice about yourself?**

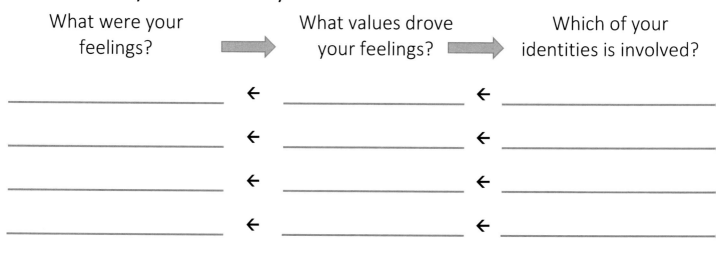

What were your feelings?		What values drove your feelings?		Which of your identities is involved?
_____	←	_____	←	_____
_____	←	_____	←	_____
_____	←	_____	←	_____
_____	←	_____	←	_____

2. **What responses did you observe from others?**

_____

_____

_____

_____

3. **Press your Pause Button. What response is most productive?**

_____

_____

_____

What's the Shape of Your Noggin?

Describe a time when you felt like an outsider.
What happened? How did you feel? What did you say or do?

_____

_____

_____

_____

Describe a time when you made someone else feel left out or unwelcome.
- What did you say or do?
- Was it intentional or done in ignorance?
- How did you feel about it at the time?
- How do you feel about it now?

_____

_____

_____

_____

_____

_____

Think of someone at work who is new to the team, or different from others in some way.

How could you start a conversation with them to help them feel included?

Affinity Bias, In-groups, and Privilege

Think about the places (real or virtual) where you interact with others in a professional setting.

What do you notice about how people organize themselves socially? Are there rigid and defined groups, does everyone mingle freely, or something in-between?

_____

_____

_____

_____

Where there are groups, consider what those individuals have in common.

For example, do they work in the same industry or have similar demographic profiles?

_____

_____

_____

_____

Do you feel comfortable in these settings?

- ❑ Yes, and I will look for people who may feel out-of-place so I can make sure they know they are welcome.
- ❑ No, and I will find someone with whom I have a common interest. I will ask that person to help me get to know others in the group.

Notes

Understand Your Personal Brand

Interview or survey at least five people with whom you have worked closely. Record their answers and look for themes.

How will you ask for input?
- ☐ Online survey
- ☐ Individual interviews
- ☐ Other format: _____

Who will you ask for input?

_____   _____

_____   _____

_____   _____

Questions to ask:
- ☐ Can you describe your experience in working with me?
- ☐ When my name comes up in the office, how do people respond?
- ☐ What's the "water cooler talk" about me / my performance / my potential?
- ☐ When have you seen me at my best?
- ☐ What one word immediately comes to mind when you think of me?
- ☐ Other:

_____

_____

_____

_____

What themes did you uncover?

_____

_____

_____

_____

What answers surprised you?

_____

_____

_____

_____

How will you use what you learned to build your personal brand?

_____

_____

_____

_____

_____

Assess Your Network

Use the instructions from Chapter 32 of *Network Beyond Bias: Making Diversity a Competitive Advantage for Your Career* to complete your assessment.

	I	G	G	N	O	R	E
C							
H							
A							
M							
P							

How do you feel about your results?

_____

_____

_____

What, if anything would you like to change?

_____

_____

_____

What is one action you can take this week to bring about the change you desire?

_____

_____

_____

How often will you re-assess your CHAMP Network?
- ❑ Quarterly
- ❑ Monthly
- ❑ Weekly
- ❑ Other: _____

Consider using the Network Like a CHAMP Networking Activity Journal _to record your conversations, meetings, and connections. The journal makes it easy to track your network in detail and periodically assess the "big picture."_

Do You Network Like a CHAMP?

Which relationships do you most need to develop?

- ❑ Customer
- ❑ Hire / Help
- ❑ Associate
- ❑ Mentor
- ❑ Protégé

Where can you find these missing connections?

_____

_____

_____

Which will be the easiest? Why?

_____

_____

Which will be most difficult? Why?

_____

_____

What will be your first step(s)?

_____

_____

Notes

What Perspectives Does Your Network IGGNORE?

In which categories do you need to be more intentional?

- ❏ Industry
- ❏ Generation
- ❏ Gender Identity
- ❏ National Origin / Native Language
- ❏ Sexual Orientation
- ❏ Race / Ethnicity

Which of these do you feel will be the most important for expanding your perspective? Why?

_____

_____

_____

_____

Do any of these categories make you uncomfortable? Why?

_____

_____

_____

_____

Where can you find these missing connections?

_____

_____

_____

_____

What will be your first step(s)?

_____

_____

Seek Different Perspectives on Purpose

1. Fill your _____ with diverse perspectives.

2. Commit to one _____ you shouldn't IGGNORE.

3. Find a _____ to stretch your thinking.

Notes

_____

_____

_____

_____

_____

_____

_____

Notes

Barriers to Inclusion

_____ is to downplay a disfavored trait to blend into the mainstream.

_____ are like papercuts we inflict upon one another, often without even realizing it.

Help others _____

by being _____ ,

_____ , and

_____ .

What identities have you noticed yourself "covering" at work? What form does your covering behavior take?

_____

_____

_____

_____

_____

What covering behaviors have you observed from others?

_____

_____

_____

_____

Is there anything you could say or do to let others know that they can be themselves around you?

_____

_____

_____

_____

Connection Requires Empathy

Think about a time you were struggling to be heard or understood. How did that feel?

_____

_____

Is there someone in your life that always "gets" you? What do they say or do that makes you feel that way?

_____

_____

How do *you* show empathy for others? Do you feel this is a strength or something you need to work on?

_____

_____

_____

_____

_____

em′ • path • y

noun

The ability to understand someone else's feelings and perspectives, and to use that understanding to guide one's own actions

Notes

What Stories Will You Tell?

Share a story from your childhood, teenage years, or early adulthood that was a defining moment for you.

What brought you to the crossroads? What core values drove your decision? What did you learn about yourself? When was the last time you told yourself or someone else this story and why?

If you are in a position of power, such as a corporate leader, think back to when you were just starting your climb up the organizational ladder.

Was there a time when you struggled to be heard or taken seriously? How did that feel? What steps did you take to cope with your environment or to change your approach? If you were in that situation today, how might you handle it differently?

_____

_____

_____

_____

_____

_____

_____

_____

_____

_____

_____

_____

Talk about times you have struggled – financially, academically, professionally, or personally.

Who helped you? What mistakes did you make? What did you learn? Do you now view this struggle as a source of embarrassment or a source of pride?

Was there ever a time you didn't fit in?

How did that feel? How has this experience influenced your leadership style?

_____

_____

_____

_____

_____

_____

_____

_____

_____

_____

_____

_____

_____

_____

_____

In what aspects of your job or life do you struggle?

When do you ask for help? Are there times when you refuse to seek help because you don't want to appear weak, incompetent, or vulnerable?

Think about a time when you missed a chance to live up to your values.

What was the situation? Why do you now feel you made the wrong decision? What options did you have, and what drove your choice? What lesson did you learn?

Talk about a time when your beliefs about something or someone were inaccurate or incomplete.

How did you become aware of your error? What work did you have to do – internally or externally – to bridge the gap? How might the situation have unfolded if you hadn't changed your mind? Did you ultimately learn more about yourself?

_____

_____

_____

_____

_____

_____

_____

_____

_____

_____

_____

_____

_____

_____

Notes

Relationships Start with Respect

res • pect'

verb

To feel or show polite or courteous responses to the wishes and judgments of others

In what way(s) do you want your colleagues to show they respect you?

_____

_____

_____

_____

_____

What are some ways you show respect to your colleagues?

_____

_____

_____

_____

Are there any relationships you'd like to start over? Describe what that would mean to you.

_____

_____

_____

_____

Notes

You Are Responsible for Your Impact

Think there's no way you're an office bully?

Ask yourself the following questions, answering each one honestly.

Check all that apply to you.

☐ In the last six months, have I told someone they're being "too sensitive" in response to something I said? Have I told anyone I work with that they "can't take a joke"?

☐ Can I remember the last time I made a joke that targeted someone's gender or gender identity, race, ethnicity, sexual orientation, or disability?

☐ Have I recently made a generalization, realized I was in "mixed company," and said, "Oh, I didn't mean *you*"?

☐ Has anyone asked me to stop making certain types of comments or called me a bully? Do people roll their eyes in exasperation?

☐ Do I feel defensive when someone points out my behavior?

☐ Do I feel like I am better / smarter / more competent than others and therefore have a *right* to denigrate them?

☐ Do I regularly exclude certain people from discussions, so I won't have to watch what I say?

What work do you have to do?

_____

_____

Do you have any apologies to make?

_____

_____

Notes

Practice Being an Ally

Which of these actions can you commit to?

- ❑ Help others feel safe in my presence by standing up for them when necessary
- ❑ Educate myself about the microaggressions experienced by different communities
- ❑ Avoid engaging in microaggressions and intervene when I observe them
- ❑ Think critically and contextually about racial bias in the media, institutional racism, and the pervasiveness of white supremacy / primacy in the dominant culture
- ❑ Think critically and contextually about gender bias in the media, institutional sexism, and the pervasiveness of male dominance in the dominant culture
- ❑ Think critically and contextually about homophobia and transphobia in the media, institutional barriers for LGBTQ people, and the pervasiveness of heteronormativity in the dominant culture
- ❑ Think critically and contextually about bias against people with disabilities in the media, the impacts of ableism, and the pervasiveness of ableism in the dominant culture
- ❑ Speak up when anyone makes a derogatory comment or joke, whether overt or subtle, regardless of the audience or the power dynamics at play
- ❑ Listen to people from marginalized groups without judgment, defensiveness, or denying their experiences
- ❑ Amplify the voices, stories, and concerns of marginalized people without speaking for them
- ❑ Notice when people are excluded from a discussion, a decision, or an opportunity, and do what I can to include them
- ❑ Pay attention to whether people from underrepresented groups seek me out as a mentor, partner, or ally, and look within myself if they do not
- ❑ Continue to educate myself about the history, contributions, challenges and oppression of minority and marginalized communities

❑ Constantly declare my *desire* to be an ally and act accordingly

❑ Wait to have the *title* of "ally" bestowed upon me by others before I consider claiming it for myself

What additional resources do you need to understand the perspectives of others who are underrepresented in the media, government, or corporate leadership?

_____

_____

Who can hold you accountable? How will you ask them to do so?

_____

_____

When Do You Feel Included?

HELLO
I FEEL INCLUDED WHEN...

www.LeadAtAnyLevel.com

HELLO
I FEEL INCLUDED WHEN...

www.LeadAtAnyLevel.com

Answers to Fill-in-the-Blank Activities

Move Beyond Unconscious Bias (page 7)

1. Put yourself on <u>notice</u>.
2. <u>Observe</u> the responses of others.
3. Press your <u>pause button.</u>

Seek Different Perspectives on Purpose (page 23)

- Fill your <u>CHAMP Network</u> with diverse perspectives.
- Commit to one <u>conversation</u> you shouldn't IGGNORE.
- Find a <u>co-mentor</u> to stretch your thinking.

Barriers to Inclusion (page 25)

- <u>Covering</u> is to downplay a disfavored trait to blend into the mainstream.
- <u>Micro-aggressions</u> are like papercuts we inflict upon one another, often without even realizing it.
- Help others <u>uncover</u> by being <u>inclusive</u>, <u>authentic</u>, and <u>vulnerable</u>.

Apply What You've Learned

Action to Take	Target Date
❑	
❑	
❑	
❑	
❑	
❑	
❑	
❑	
❑	
❑	
❑	
❑	
❑	

Also Available from Amy C. Waninger

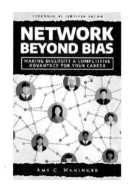

Network Beyond Bias: Making Diversity a Competitive Advantage for Your Career

Copyright © 2018 by Amy C. Waninger

ISBN: 978-1-718681-51-4

LCCN: 2018906105

Network Like a CHAMP: Networking Activity Journal

Copyright © 2018 by Amy C. Waninger

ISBN: 978-1-726659-95-6

Hire Beyond Bias: How to Pick the Best Person for the Job

Copyright © 2019 by Amy C. Waninger

ISBN: : 978-1-793226-88-4